The Power of AI
How to Utilize Artificial Intelligence for Sales Success

Theodore Staple

IMC Sales Management & Publishing Inc.

INTRODUCTION

Welcome to "The Power of AI: How to Utilize Artificial Intelligence for Sales Success"! In today's rapidly evolving business landscape, sales professionals need every advantage they can get to stay ahead of the curve and succeed. And that's where AI comes in. Artificial intelligence is revolutionizing the way we approach sales, from personalized messaging and intelligent lead generation to predictive analytics and automated workflows. But with so much buzz and hype around AI, it can be difficult to know where to start or how to integrate it into your sales strategy.

That's where this book comes in. We've gathered insights and expertise from top sales professionals and AI experts to give you a comprehensive guide to leveraging AI for sales success. Whether you're a sales executive looking to drive revenue growth or a sales rep wanting to improve your performance, this book has something for you. You'll learn about the latest AI technologies and applications, and how they can be used to supercharge your sales strategy. You'll also discover practical tips, case studies, and best practices for implementing AI in your sales process.

You will note some common themes and concepts throughout this book. Each chapter is structure as a check list of concepts to consider at each stage of your development and understanding of AI's application in the sales environment. Please excuse these redundancies, they are critical components that need to be considered at many points within your AI journey.

So, if you're ready to unlock the power of AI and take your sales game to the next level, let's get started!

CHAPTER 1:

THE RISE OF AI IN SALES

Artificial intelligence has become one of the hottest topics in the sales world in recent years. It's no wonder why - AI has the potential to transform the way we approach sales, making it more efficient, effective, and personalized. But how did we get here? In this chapter, we'll explore the rise of AI in sales and how it has evolved over time.

AI has been around for decades, but it's only in the last few years that it has started to gain mainstream acceptance and usage. One of the main reasons for this is the sheer amount of data that is available today. With the proliferation of digital devices and the rise of the internet, businesses now have access to vast amounts of data about their customers and prospects. This data can be used to train AI models and make more accurate predictions about customer behavior, preferences, and needs.

Another reason for the rise of AI in sales is the increasing demand for personalized experiences. Today's customers expect businesses to understand their unique needs and preferences and tailor their interactions accordingly. AI can help sales reps do this at scale, by analyzing customer data and making recommendations for personalized messaging and offerings.

AI is also being used to automate routine tasks and free up sales reps to focus on high-value activities, such as building relationships and closing deals. For example, chatbots can be used to handle customer inquiries and provide support, while automated lead scoring and prioritization can help reps focus their time on the most promising opportunities.

As AI technology continues to evolve and become more sophisticated, its potential in the sales world is only going to grow. In the next chapter, we'll explore the different types of AI and how they can be applied in sales contexts.

CHAPTER 2:

TYPES OF AI IN SALES

Not all AI is created equal. In fact, there are several different types of AI, each with its own strengths and weaknesses. In this chapter, we'll explore the different types of AI and how they can be applied in sales contexts.

Rule-Based Ai

This type of AI relies on a set of predefined rules to make decisions. It's commonly used in chatbots and virtual assistants, where the AI follows a script to respond to customer inquiries. While rule-based AI can be effective for simple tasks, it's limited in its ability to handle complex situations and adapt to changing circumstances.

Machine Learning:

Machine learning is a type of AI that involves training algorithms on large amounts of data to identify patterns and make predictions. In sales, machine learning can be used for tasks like lead scoring, where the AI analyzes historical data to identify the characteristics of high-quality leads and prioritize them accordingly.

Deep Learning

Deep learning is a subset of machine learning that uses neural networks to model complex relationships between data points. It's often used in applications like image recognition and natural language processing. In sales, deep learning can be used to analyze unstructured data like customer conversations and social media posts to identify patterns and insights.

Natural Language Processing (Nlp)

NLP is a type of AI that enables computers to understand and interpret human language. It's commonly used in chatbots and virtual assistants to provide personalized responses to customer inquiries. In sales, NLP can be used to analyze customer conversations and identify key topics and sentiment.

Predictive Analytics

Predictive analytics is a type of AI that uses statistical models to make predictions about future outcomes based on historical data. In sales, predictive analytics can be used for tasks like forecasting revenue and identifying the most promising leads.

Each of these types of AI has its own strengths and weaknesses, and they can be used in combination to create powerful sales solutions. In the next chapter, we'll explore some of the specific use cases for AI in sales.

CHAPTER 3:
USE CASES FOR AI IN SALES

In this chapter, we'll explore some of the specific ways that AI can be used in sales to improve efficiency, accuracy, and effectiveness.

Lead Scoring

One of the most common use cases for AI in sales is lead scoring. By analyzing historical data on closed deals, AI algorithms can identify the characteristics of high-quality leads and prioritize them accordingly. This allows sales teams to focus their efforts on the most promising leads, improving their chances of success.

Sales Forecasting

AI can also be used to predict future sales outcomes based on historical data. By analyzing trends in customer behavior, market conditions, and other factors, AI algorithms can generate accurate forecasts of future revenue. This allows sales teams to make more informed decisions about resource allocation and strategy.

Chatbots And Virtual Assistants

Chatbots and virtual assistants are becoming increasingly popular in sales, as they can provide personalized support to customers 24/7. By using natural language processing and other AI technologies, these tools can understand customer inquiries and provide helpful responses in real-time. This can improve customer satisfaction and reduce the workload on sales teams.

Personalization

AI can also be used to personalize the sales experience for individual customers. By analyzing data on customer behavior and preferences, AI algorithms can recommend products and services that are likely to be of interest to them. This can improve the chances of making a sale and build customer loyalty over time.

Sales Coaching

AI can also be used to coach sales reps and provide feedback on their performance. By analyzing data on customer interactions, AI algorithms can identify areas where reps are excelling and areas where they need improvement. This can help sales teams to identify best practices and improve their overall performance.

Pricing Optimization

AI can also be used to optimize pricing strategies based on customer behavior and market conditions. By analyzing data on customer buying patterns and competitive offerings, AI algorithms can recommend prices that are likely to maximize revenue while remaining competitive in the market.

These are just a few of the many ways that AI can be used in sales. As AI technologies continue to evolve and become more sophisticated, we can expect to see even more innovative use cases emerge in the coming years. In the next chapter, we'll explore some of the potential benefits and challenges of using AI in sales.

CHAPTER 4:

BENEFITS AND CHALLENGES OF USING AI IN SALES

In this chapter, we'll explore some of the potential benefits and challenges of using AI in sales.

BENEFITS:

Increased Efficiency

AI can automate many routine tasks, such as lead scoring and data entry, allowing sales reps to focus on higher-level tasks that require more strategic thinking.

Improved Accuracy

AI algorithms can analyze vast amounts of data quickly and accurately, providing insights that may be missed by human analysts

Personalization

AI can analyze customer data to provide personalized recommendations and support, improving the overall customer experience and building loyalty.

Sales Forecasting

AI can provide accurate sales forecasts based on historical data, helping sales teams to make more informed decisions about resource allocation and strategy.

Competitive Advantage

Sales teams that use AI can gain a competitive advantage by making more informed decisions, improving the accuracy of their forecasts, and providing better customer support.

CHALLENGES:

Implementation Costs

Implementing AI technologies can be costly, and may require significant investment in infrastructure and training.

Data Quality

AI algorithms require high-quality data to operate effectively, and many organizations struggle with data quality issues.

Ethical Concerns

There are concerns around the use of AI in sales, particularly around privacy and data security.

Resistance To Change

Some sales reps may be resistant to using AI technologies, and may require significant training to become proficient.

Over-Reliance On Technology

Sales teams that rely too heavily on AI technologies may miss opportunities for human connection and relationship-building, which are critical in sales.

Overall, the benefits of using AI in sales are significant, but organizations must also be mindful of the potential challenges and risks. By carefully evaluating their needs and capabilities, organizations can implement AI technologies in a way that maximizes the benefits while minimizing the risks. In the next chapter, we'll explore some of the best practices for implementing AI in sales.

CHAPTER 5:

BEST PRACTICES FOR IMPLEMENTING AI IN SALES

In this chapter, we'll explore some of the best practices for implementing AI in sales.

Identify Areas For Automation

Before implementing AI technologies, it's important to identify the areas of your sales process that can benefit the most from automation. This could include lead scoring, data entry, or sales forecasting, among others.

Start Small

Rather than trying to implement AI across your entire sales process at once, start with a small pilot project to test the technology and identify any issues that may arise.

Invest In Data Quality

To get the most out of AI technologies, it's critical to have high-quality data. Invest in data quality initiatives, such as data cleansing and standardization, to ensure that your data is accurate and reliable.

Train Your Team

Sales reps will need to be trained on how to use AI technologies effectively. This includes understanding how the technology works, what data is required, and how to interpret the insights provided by the technology.

Monitor And Measure Results

As with any new technology, it's important to monitor and measure the results of your AI implementation. This will help you to identify areas for improvement and ensure that you are getting the most out of your investment.

Address Ethical Concerns

As we discussed in Chapter 4, there are ethical concerns around the use of AI in sales. It's important to have clear policies in place around data privacy and security, and to ensure that your AI technologies are being used in an ethical and responsible manner.

Foster Collaboration

AI technologies should be seen as a tool to support sales reps, not replace them. Foster collaboration between sales reps and AI technologies to ensure that both are working together effectively.

By following these best practices, organizations can implement AI technologies in a way that maximizes the benefits and minimizes the risks. In the next chapter, we'll explore some of the emerging trends in AI for sales and what they mean for the future of sales.

CHAPTER 6:

EMERGING TRENDS IN AI FOR SALES

In this chapter, we'll take a look at some of the emerging trends in AI for sales and what they mean for the future of sales.

Conversational Ai

One of the biggest trends in AI for sales is conversational AI, which uses natural language processing to allow sales reps to have more natural and productive conversations with customers. With conversational AI, sales reps can get real-time insights and recommendations to help them better understand the customer's needs and provide more personalized recommendations.

Predictive Analytics

Another emerging trend in AI for sales is predictive analytics, which uses machine learning algorithms to analyze customer data and predict future behavior. With predictive analytics, sales reps can identify which customers are most likely to buy, what products they are most likely to buy, and when they are most likely to buy.

Automated Lead Nurturing

AI technologies can also be used to automate lead nurturing, allowing sales reps to focus on the most promising leads. By automating lead nurturing, sales reps can ensure that they are staying in touch with leads and providing them with the information they need to make a purchasing decision.

Augmented Reality

Augmented reality is another emerging trend in AI for sales, which allows customers to visualize products in a more immersive and interactive way. With augmented reality, customers can see how products would look in their home or office, which can help to increase sales and reduce returns.

Sales Coaching

AI technologies can also be used to provide sales coaching, giving reps real-time feedback and suggestions on how to improve their sales pitch. This can help to improve the effectiveness of the sales team and increase overall sales.

These are just a few of the emerging trends in AI for sales, and we can expect to see many more in the coming years. As AI technologies continue to improve and become more accessible, they will become an increasingly important tool for sales teams looking to improve their performance and stay ahead of the competition.

CHAPTER 7:

CHALLENGES AND LIMITATIONS OF AI FOR SALES

While AI technologies offer many benefits for sales teams, there are also some challenges and limitations that need to be considered. In this chapter, we'll explore some of the challenges and limitations of AI for sales.

Data Quality

One of the biggest challenges of AI for sales is data quality. AI relies on high-quality data to make accurate predictions and recommendations, and if the data is incomplete or inaccurate, the results can be unreliable.

Lack Of Human Touch

Another challenge of AI for sales is the lack of human touch. While AI can provide valuable insights and recommendations, it can't replace the personal touch and relationship-building skills that are essential in sales.

Cost

Implementing AI technologies can be expensive, and not all sales teams may have the budget to invest in these tools.

Resistance To Change

Some sales reps may be resistant to using AI technologies, either because they don't understand how they work or because they feel threatened by the idea of automation.

Ethical Considerations

AI technologies raise important ethical considerations, such as privacy concerns and the potential for bias in the data and algorithms.

Complexity

AI technologies can be complex and require specialized expertise to implement and maintain, which can be a challenge for some sales teams.

Limited Scope

AI technologies are not a panacea for all sales-related issues, and there are some tasks and situations where human intuition and creativity may be more effective.

Overall, while AI technologies offer many benefits for sales teams, it's important to be aware of these challenges and limitations and to approach their implementation with careful consideration and planning. By addressing these challenges and limitations, sales teams can maximize the benefits of AI technologies while minimizing their drawbacks.

CHAPTER 8:

THE FUTURE OF AI FOR SALES

AI technologies have already had a significant impact on sales, and their role is only going to become more important in the years ahead. In this chapter, we'll explore some of the trends and predictions for the future of AI in sales.

Personalization

One of the most promising areas for AI in sales is personalization. By analyzing customer data, AI algorithms can provide highly personalized recommendations and offers, improving the customer experience and driving sales.

Chatbots And Virtual Assistants

Chatbots and virtual assistants are already being used in many industries, and they are likely to become even more prevalent in sales. These tools can provide customers with instant support and answers to their questions, improving satisfaction and reducing the workload for sales reps.

Sales Forecasting

AI can be used to analyze sales data and make accurate sales forecasts, helping sales teams to make better decisions and allocate resources more effectively.

Automation

AI technologies can automate many routine and repetitive tasks, freeing up sales reps to focus on more strategic and creative work.

Augmented Intelligence

The future of AI in sales is likely to involve more sophisticated forms of augmented intelligence, where AI technologies work in collaboration with human sales reps to provide insights and recommendations.

Integration With Other Technologies

AI technologies are likely to become more integrated with other sales technologies, such as CRM systems, marketing automation platforms, and e-commerce platforms, providing a more seamless and holistic sales experience.

Ethical Considerations

As the role of AI in sales becomes more important, it will be essential to address important ethical considerations, such as data privacy, bias, and transparency.

Overall, the future of AI in sales looks bright, with many exciting possibilities for improving the customer experience, streamlining sales processes, and driving revenue growth. By staying up-to-date on the latest trends and best practices, sales teams can take full advantage of the power of AI to achieve their goals and stay ahead of the competition.

CHAPTER 9:

OVERCOMING CHALLENGES AND BARRIERS

While the potential benefits of AI for sales are clear, there are also a number of challenges and barriers that must be overcome. In this chapter, we'll explore some of the most significant challenges and provide strategies for addressing them.

Data Quality

AI algorithms require large amounts of high-quality data to function effectively. Poor data quality can lead to inaccurate predictions and recommendations. To overcome this challenge, sales teams must invest in data quality and management processes, ensuring that their data is accurate, up-to-date, and properly stored.

Integration With Existing Systems

AI technologies must be integrated with existing sales systems, such as CRM platforms and marketing automation tools, to be effective. However, integration can be challenging, particularly if different systems use different data formats or standards. Sales teams must work closely with their IT departments and vendors to ensure smooth integration.

Adoption By Sales Reps

While AI technologies can automate many routine tasks and provide valuable insights, they can also be intimidating or difficult to use for some sales reps. Sales teams must provide training and support to help their reps understand and use AI tools effectively.

Ethical Considerations

As we discussed in the previous chapter, there are important ethical considerations related to the use of AI in sales. Sales teams must be aware of these issues and take steps to ensure that their use of AI is transparent, fair, and respectful of customer privacy.

By addressing these challenges, sales teams can overcome barriers to AI adoption and fully realize the benefits of AI for sales. This may require significant investment in technology, data quality, and training, but the potential rewards in terms of improved sales performance and customer satisfaction can be substantial.

CHAPTER 10:

THE FUTURE OF AI IN SALES

As AI technologies continue to advance, their potential for sales is only expected to grow. In this chapter, we'll explore some of the exciting possibilities for the future of AI in sales.

Personalization

AI can be used to personalize sales interactions based on customer data and behavior. By analyzing customer interactions and preferences, AI algorithms can recommend products, tailor marketing messages, and provide a more personalized sales experience.

Predictive Analytics

AI can be used to analyze large datasets and make predictions about future sales trends and customer behavior. By identifying patterns and trends in customer data, AI algorithms can help sales teams anticipate customer needs and make more informed sales decisions.

Sales Forecasting

AI can be used to predict sales outcomes based on historical data, market trends, and other factors. By providing accurate sales forecasts, AI algorithms can help sales teams better plan and manage their sales efforts.

Chatbots And Virtual Assistants

AI-powered chatbots and virtual assistants can help automate routine sales tasks, such as answering customer questions and scheduling appointments. By handling these tasks, sales reps can focus on higher-value sales activities.

Sales Coaching

AI can be used to provide sales coaching and training, analyzing sales calls and providing feedback on areas for improvement. This can help sales reps improve their performance and achieve better results.

These are just a few examples of the exciting possibilities for the future of AI in sales. As AI technologies continue to evolve and become more sophisticated, they are likely to transform the way that sales teams operate, leading to more efficient and effective sales processes, and ultimately better customer outcomes.

CHAPTER 11:

THE ETHICS OF AI IN SALES

While the potential benefits of AI in sales are significant, it's also important to consider the ethical implications of its use. In this chapter, we'll explore some of the ethical considerations that sales teams should keep in mind when using AI.

Privacy

AI algorithms rely on customer data to personalize sales interactions and make predictions about customer behavior. However, it's important to ensure that this data is collected and used ethically, with customer consent and in accordance with applicable laws and regulations.

Bias

AI algorithms can unintentionally perpetuate biases if they are trained on biased datasets. It's important to ensure that AI algorithms are trained on diverse and representative datasets, and that they are regularly monitored and audited to detect and correct for bias.

Transparency

It's important for sales teams to be transparent about their use of AI, both with customers and with their own employees. Customers should be informed about how their data is being used, and sales reps should be trained on how to use AI ethically and transparently.

Accountability

Sales teams should be accountable for the decisions made by their AI algorithms. This means that they should be able to explain how their AI algorithms work, and should be able to demonstrate that their algorithms are producing ethical outcomes.

Human Oversight

While AI can be used to automate many sales tasks, it's important to ensure that there is still human oversight and intervention when necessary. This can help prevent errors and ensure that ethical considerations are being taken into account.

By keeping these ethical considerations in mind, sales teams can ensure that their use of AI is responsible, ethical, and aligned with the values of their organization and their customers.

CHAPTER 12:

BEST PRACTICES FOR AI IMPLEMENTATION IN SALES

Now that we've explored the potential benefits and ethical considerations of AI in sales, let's take a look at some best practices for implementing AI in your sales strategy.

Start With Clear Goals

Before implementing AI, it's important to have a clear understanding of the business goals you want to achieve. This will help you determine which AI tools and techniques are best suited to your needs.

Choose The Right Technology

There are a wide range of AI tools and technologies available, and it's important to choose the ones that are best suited to your specific sales needs. Consider factors such as data volume and quality, model complexity, and ease of integration with your existing sales tools.

Collect High-Quality Data

AI algorithms rely on high-quality data to make accurate predictions and recommendations. Make sure that you are collecting relevant, accurate, and comprehensive data from a variety of sources.

Train Your Algorithms Well

The accuracy and effectiveness of your AI algorithms will depend largely on the quality of their training data. Make sure that you are using diverse and representative data sets to train your algorithms, and that you are regularly monitoring and retraining them to ensure optimal performance.

Ensure Transparency And Accountability

Be transparent with your customers about how you are using AI in your sales interactions, and be accountable for the decisions made by your AI algorithms. This can help build trust with customers and ensure ethical use of AI.

Provide Human Oversight

While AI can automate many sales tasks, it's important to have human oversight and intervention when necessary. This can help prevent errors and ensure that ethical considerations are being taken into account.

Measure And Track Results

Monitor the performance of your AI algorithms and track key metrics such as sales conversions, customer satisfaction, and revenue. Use this data to continuously optimize your AI sales strategy over time.

By following these best practices, sales teams can successfully implement AI in their sales strategy and achieve significant benefits, while also ensuring that they are using AI in an ethical and responsible manner.

CHAPTER 13:

CASE STUDIES OF AI IN SALES

To gain a better understanding of how AI is being used in sales today, let's take a look at some real-world case studies.

Salesforce Einstein

Salesforce Einstein is an AI-powered tool that provides sales teams with personalized recommendations on which leads to pursue and which sales tactics to use. The tool analyzes data from a variety of sources, including email and social media, to help sales reps prioritize their efforts and close more deals.

Gong.io

Gong.io is a conversational analytics tool that uses AI to analyze sales calls and provide real-time feedback to sales reps. The tool helps sales teams identify common objections and areas for improvement, and provides recommendations on how to best respond to specific customer concerns.

Insidesales.com

InsideSales.com uses AI to predict which leads are most likely to convert, and provides sales teams with personalized recommendations on how to engage with those leads. The tool analyzes data from a variety of sources, including email and social media, to identify patterns and make predictions about future customer behavior.

Conversica

Conversica is an AI-powered sales assistant that automates lead engagement and follow-up. The tool uses natural language processing to engage with leads in a conversational manner, and can handle tasks such as scheduling appointments and answering common questions.

Hootsuite Insights

Hootsuite Insights is an AI-powered tool that helps sales teams monitor social media conversations about their brand and industry. The tool analyzes data from social media platforms such as Twitter and Instagram, and provides insights on trends, sentiment, and customer feedback.

These case studies demonstrate the wide range of applications for AI in sales, from lead prioritization to conversational analytics and social media monitoring. By leveraging AI tools and technologies, sales teams can gain valuable insights and streamline their sales processes to drive greater revenue and customer satisfaction.

CHAPTER 14:

CHALLENGES AND CONSIDERATIONS FOR IMPLEMENTING AI IN SALES

While there are many benefits to implementing AI in sales, there are also some challenges and considerations to keep in mind. In this chapter, we'll take a look at some of the key challenges and considerations for businesses looking to adopt AI in their sales processes.

Data Quality

One of the biggest challenges for implementing AI in sales is ensuring that the data being used is accurate and high-quality. AI algorithms rely on data to make predictions and recommendations, so if the data is incomplete or inaccurate, it can lead to flawed insights and decision-making.

Integration With Existing Systems

Another challenge is integrating AI tools with existing sales systems and processes. This requires careful planning and coordination to ensure that the AI tools work seamlessly with existing systems and do not disrupt sales operations.

User Adoption

AI tools are only effective if they are used regularly and correctly by sales teams. However, some sales reps may be resistant to using new tools and technologies, particularly if they are seen as replacing human intuition and judgment.

Ethical Considerations

AI in sales raises ethical considerations, particularly around privacy and bias. For example, using AI to analyze social media data may raise privacy concerns, while using AI to make hiring decisions could perpetuate bias if the algorithm is not designed to be neutral and inclusive.

Cost And Roi

Implementing AI in sales can be costly, particularly for smaller businesses that may not have the resources to invest in sophisticated AI tools. It's important to carefully evaluate the potential return on investment (ROI) and weigh the costs against the expected benefits.

Overall, implementing AI in sales requires careful planning and consideration, and should be approached with a clear understanding of the potential benefits and challenges. By addressing these challenges proactively, businesses can ensure a successful and effective implementation of AI in their sales processes.

CHAPTER 15:

FUTURE OF AI IN SALES

As AI continues to evolve and become more sophisticated, its role in sales is likely to become even more important. In this chapter, we'll take a look at some of the future trends and possibilities for AI in sales.

Personalization

AI has the potential to help sales teams deliver more personalized experiences to customers. By analyzing customer data and behavior, AI algorithms can recommend products and services that are tailored to each individual customer's needs and preferences.

Predictive Analytics

AI can help sales teams make more accurate predictions about customer behavior and preferences. By analyzing historical data, AI algorithms can identify patterns and trends that can help sales teams make more informed decisions about which products to offer, which leads to pursue, and which sales tactics are most effective.

Sales Coaching

AI can also be used to coach and train sales reps. By analyzing calls and other interactions, AI algorithms can provide feedback and coaching to help sales reps improve their communication skills and become more effective at closing deals.

Chatbots

AI-powered chatbots can help businesses automate customer service and sales interactions, providing customers with quick and convenient assistance 24/7.

Enhanced Efficiency

AI can help sales teams become more efficient and effective by automating repetitive tasks, such as data entry and lead qualification, freeing up sales reps to focus on more high-value activities, such as building relationships with customers.

Overall, the future of AI in sales is exciting and full of possibilities. As AI technology continues to advance, businesses that are able to harness its power will be better equipped to meet the evolving needs of customers and stay ahead of the competition.

CHAPTER 16:

ETHICAL CONSIDERATIONS IN AI SALES

While the benefits of AI in sales are clear, it's also important to consider the ethical implications of its use. In this chapter, we'll explore some of the key ethical considerations that businesses should keep in mind when utilizing AI in their sales efforts.

Transparency

One of the most important ethical considerations in AI sales is transparency. Businesses must be transparent about how they are using AI to make sales decisions and how the algorithms are making those decisions. This includes being open about the data that is being used to train the algorithms and how that data is being collected.

Bias

Another key ethical concern in AI sales is bias. AI algorithms can inadvertently perpetuate biases that exist in the data that is used to train them. This can result in unfair treatment of certain groups of people or the exclusion of certain groups from sales opportunities.

Privacy

AI sales tools may collect and process large amounts of personal data, which raises concerns about privacy. Businesses must ensure that they are collecting only the data that is necessary for their sales efforts and that they are protecting that data in accordance with relevant laws and regulations.

Accountability

Businesses must also ensure that they are accountable for the actions of their AI systems. This includes being able to explain how decisions were made and taking responsibility for any negative impacts that may result from those decisions.

Human Oversight

Finally, businesses must ensure that there is human oversight of their AI sales systems. While AI can be incredibly powerful, it's not infallible, and there may be situations where human judgment is necessary to make the right decision.

By considering these ethical concerns and taking steps to address them, businesses can ensure that their use of AI in sales is responsible, fair, and effective.

CHAPTER 17:

TOP 20 QUESTIONS PEOPLE ASK ABOUT AI SALES

In this chapter, we'll answer some of the most common questions people have about AI in sales.

What is AI in sales?
AI in sales refers to the use of artificial intelligence technologies to improve sales processes, such as lead generation, customer segmentation, and sales forecasting.

How does AI help with sales?
AI can help with sales by analyzing large amounts of data to identify patterns and insights that can inform sales decisions, such as which leads are most likely to convert or which products are most likely to sell.

What are some examples of AI in sales?
Examples of AI in sales include chatbots, lead scoring algorithms, and predictive analytics tools.

Can AI replace salespeople?
While AI can automate some sales processes, such as lead generation, it cannot replace the human touch that is often necessary to close a sale. Salespeople still play a critical role in building relationships with customers and closing deals.

How does AI affect sales job opportunities?
While AI may automate some sales processes, it also creates new job opportunities in fields such as data analysis and AI development.

Is AI in sales ethical?
The use of AI in sales raises ethical concerns around transparency, bias, privacy, accountability, and human oversight. Businesses must take steps to ensure that their use of AI in sales is responsible, fair, and effective.

Can AI help with customer segmentation?
Yes, AI can analyze customer data to segment customers based on their behavior, demographics, and preferences.

How can AI help with lead generation?
AI can help with lead generation by analyzing data to identify which leads are most likely to convert and providing insights on how to target those leads effectively.

Can AI predict sales outcomes?
Yes, AI can use predictive analytics to forecast sales outcomes based on historical data and other factors.

How can businesses implement AI in their sales processes?
Businesses can implement AI in their sales processes by identifying areas where AI can improve efficiency and effectiveness, selecting appropriate AI tools, and ensuring that they have the necessary data and resources to train and maintain those tools.

Can AI help with sales forecasting?
Yes, AI can use predictive analytics to forecast sales outcomes and help businesses make data-driven decisions.

Can AI be used to personalize sales experiences?
Yes, AI can analyze customer data to provide personalized product recommendations and targeted marketing messages.

How can businesses ensure that their AI systems are unbiased?
Businesses can ensure that their AI systems are unbiased by regularly reviewing and auditing the data used to train those systems and implementing measures to mitigate any biases that are identified.

Can AI improve customer satisfaction?
Yes, AI can help businesses provide faster and more personalized customer service, which can improve customer satisfaction.

Can AI help with sales team performance?
Yes, AI can provide sales teams with data-driven insights and recommendations that can help them improve their performance.

How can businesses measure the ROI of AI in sales?
Businesses can measure the ROI of AI in sales by tracking metrics such as lead conversion rates, customer retention rates, and sales revenue.

How can businesses ensure that their use of AI in sales is compliant with data privacy regulations?
Businesses can ensure that their use of AI in sales is compliant with data privacy regulations by implementing appropriate data collection, processing, and storage measures and obtaining necessary consents from customers.

Can AI help businesses identify upselling and cross-selling opportunities?
Yes, AI can analyze customer data to identify opportunities for upselling and cross-selling.

How can businesses ensure that their AI systems are transparent?
Businesses can ensure that their AI systems are transparent by documenting the algorithms used to make decisions, providing explanations for those decisions, and allowing customers to access and correct

IN CLOSING.

Utlizing AI effectively and strategically can increase your sales efficency, accuracy, close rate, and overall sales volume without increasing cost-of-sales. The right strategic approach to the utilization of AI within sales processes will dicate the growth in this sector. Effectively strategies in this regard will be what seperates the successful sale organizations from the pack in the coming month and years.

The knowledge you have acquired within the pages of this book is your head start. Don't waste it. Good luck, and good selling!

Printed in Great Britain
by Amazon

27245328R10030